ACHES
& PAINS

By Maeve Binchy

Light a Penny Candle
Echoes
London Transports
Dublin 4
The Lilac Bus
Firefly Summer
Silver Wedding
Circle of Friends
The Copper Beech
The Glass Lake
Evening Class
Tara Road
Scarlet Feather
Aches & Pains (non-fiction)
Cross Lines (short stories)
Quentins (short stories)

Illustrated by Wendy Shea

Hell, Said the Duchess by Gemma O'Connor
The Cool MacCool by Gordon Snell
Hysterically Historical by Gordon Snell
Exquisite Manners by Maureen Cairn-Duff
Dublin Shopping Guide by Deirdre McQuillan
Aches & Pains by Maeve Binchy

ACHES & PAINS

MAEVE BINCHY

Illustrated by WENDY SHEA

ORION

An Orion paperback

First published in Great Britain in 1999
by Orion Books Ltd,
Orion House, 5 Upper St Martin's Lane,
London WC2H 9EA

Third impression
Reissued 2002
Copyright © Maeve Binchy 1999
Illustrations copyright © Wendy Shea 1999

The right of Maeve Binchy and Wendy Shea
to be identified as the author of this work has
been asserted by them in accordance with the
Copyright, Designs and Patents Act 1988.

A CIP catalogue record for this book is available
from the British Library.

ISBN 0 75284 863 1

Printed and bound in Great Britain by
Clays Ltd, St Ives plc

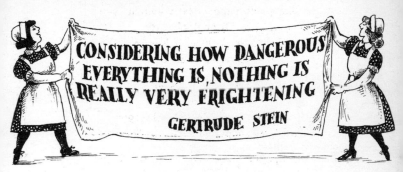

CONSIDERING HOW DANGEROUS EVERYTHING IS, NOTHING IS REALLY VERY FRIGHTENING

GERTRUDE STEIN

*For dear Gordon, and all the other
good people who made me better.*

MAEVE BINCHY

For Freida and Eileen - there's only one of each.

WENDY SHEA

ACHES & PAINS

This is a 'Cheer up' book. Not 'Cheer up, it may never happen' . . . because to some extent it has happened. You're not well. Not 'Cheer up because there are people much worse off'. That is a ludicrous piece of advice. Are we seriously meant to feel better when told someone else is in bad shape? Not 'Cheer up because the rest of us are sick of looking at your misery-ridden face and you're actually depressing everyone in a radius of five kilometres'.

It's really a sort of survival manual: some nanny-ish advice about how to muddle through a time of aches and pains. There's also a slight touch of the head girl mentality in it, I think. And though neither Wendy Shea nor I were ever head girl material, we have each long had this feeling that we could run the universe quite adequately if asked to in a polite tone of voice.

Not that either of us is a very good role model for anyone with aches and pains. There was an awful lot of grizzling and anxious whingeing as we both packed our suitcases and went off, hearts pounding, to different hospitals to get hip replacements. No medals for bravery were pinned to either of our nighties during our stay in hospital.

But on the other hand, things weren't nearly as bad as we thought they would be. You can get used to anything after a while, and I am still automatically offering my arm every time I see anyone in uniform, expecting to have it wrapped up while blood pressure is taken or stuck with needles while blood is injected or removed. I've offered my arm to air stewardesses and cinema ushers and security guards in a kind of reflex reaction, but so far none of them has taken me up on it.

I was very interested in other people in hospital, and had amazing conversations in the corridors with total strangers as I limped around with them. Together we would study the hip manual and note that sexual intercourse could be attempted after so many weeks, which was a good topic of conversation at the water cooler. The hip manual also said that after eight weeks we should be able to drive.

'That's great,' one man said wistfully. 'I always wanted to know how to drive but I never had time to learn, it will be a huge advantage to me.'

Wendy and I both met, in our separate hospitals, fellow patients who were optimistic, cheerful and interested in others. We also met people with weaselish bad tempers who were driving their families insane, and gloomboots who thought no medication was working and suspected incipient clots in every part of their body. We met those frightened that they would-n't get cured and get back to work, and those who were already malingering and plotting scams to stay out longer.

We learned awful things about healthy eating plans, and good posture and the amount of exercise that normal people are meant to take.

And Wendy and I both got a whole new lease of life from the new legs, and wanted, as a thank-you, to try to raise some funds to support the good work of the Arthritis Research Campaign, which you are helping to do by buying this book.

But we also wanted to pass on the wisdom that the cheerful survive somehow better and help themselves as well as everyone else along the way. The wallowing in other people's sympathy doesn't do all that much to make you feel better. How many times do you want anyone to say 'How terrible it must be for you'?

Everyone is different, and of course there are people for whom the ultra-sympathetic tones and hours of listening to their ailments are what will make them better. Speaking personally, I'd be afraid to risk it.

It's not that I wasn't grateful for sympathy during two years of great pain and much disablement before the operation. I suppose I'm afraid the sympathy fuse is short and can be tried to breaking point, so I allowed myself to indulge in it very sparingly. I said I was fine when I was terrible, and I was much better when I was much worse, and I was full of hope when I was glum with despair.

It worked so well that some people said there was nothing at all wrong with me, except that I seemed for some reason to be bent double, walking on two sticks, yelping a bit and unable to climb three steps. Others, who knew there was quite a bit more to it, realised that this was the way I wanted to play it and went along with it. So not only did I see good humour and optimism reflected in the faces I looked at, which was immensely cheering, but the approach worked when I was alone. I had said so often that I was great I almost believed it myself. And on the odd day when I really did need the shoulder to wail on I felt I could ask for it because it wasn't already sodden with the damp of a thousand wails.

I admit that after the operation, I didn't want people to be brisk and dismissive either, saying 'Nonsense, there's nothing to it', when they stood there on their two good legs and I had a contraption tied to me to make sure I didn't lie on my side by accident. I didn't want them to minimise it, and say that everyone, including the dogs in the street, were having these joint replacements all the time these days.

And I certainly didn't like being offered the healing power of crystals, the address of a seventh son of a seventh son, a pounded mixture of herbs to apply to the afflicted part, a copper anklet or a mantra never known to fail.

What *did* I want then?

I suppose like anyone I wanted to be treated with concern and affection, but most of all to be treated as if things were normal, as they had once been, and would be again not so very far in the future.

If that's what you want, how do you get people to

treat you like that? The good news is that it's the invalid who calls the shots. All we have to do if we want to avoid sepulchral sympathy, remorseless heartiness or off-the-wall cures – whichever is most maddening – is to send out the right vibes.

I'm not at all suggesting we ignore symptoms, refuse treatment and abandon everything that modern medicine can do for us. Absolutely the contrary. We should seek advice early and then take it. We should rejoice that we live after rather than during the days of leeches and bleedings and dosing with unmentionable things. If ever there was a reason not to mourn the passing of the good old days, it would be in terms of health.

Nor is this book about putting on a show for the visitor. It's about coming to terms with the fact that our bodies are not invincible after all; realising that we are not toddlers who have fallen over and will get up ten seconds later to waddle on.

It's only human to be anxious and doubtful and sometimes just outraged that parts of us aren't working properly. We vow that if only this pain or that ache would go then we will never complain again. We spend futile hours looking back on a mis-spent life and blaming ourselves for whatever has befallen us.

This is natural. There's really no such thing as a naturally good patient. Who is able to be genuinely good-tempered through wheezes and snuffles and fractures and labour pains and attacks of nausea? But eventually, we probably learn to be slightly better patients than we feel like being. Partly for social survival, but partly for sheer self-preservation, we learn to cheer up.

I hope that there is something in this book that will cheer you up. Not too boisterously, as if a manic face were two inches from yours saying menacingly, 'You will be good-humoured or else'. I have met too many professional Pollyannas in my life to think that good humour can be imposed on people successfully.

And I hope nothing in this book will suggest that it was written and illustrated by two people with a huge history of courage and stoicism. In fact, the next time either of us are poorly, we may well have to consult ourselves here to recall why we were so over-confident as to produce a manual advising all around us on attitude and behaviour.

But it is written with great sympathy, a fairly light heart and a genuine belief that nothing is quite as bad as it seems at four o'clock in the morning.

MAEVE BINCHY

ACHES
& PAINS

BARING YOUR BODY

Did anyone ever say that going for a medical examination is somehow in the same league as entering a beauty competition?

Yet nurses say they are driven mad by time-wasting false modesty, and insanely apologetic attitudes about what is, after all, just a human body. Although sympathetic and aware of how low some people's self-esteem can be, particularly at a time of ill health, medical staff say they often wish there was some kind of basic training course for patients, something to convince them that this is not an exhibition or a peep show. It's an attempt to find out what is wrong with them and cure it.

They report patients who clutch onto hospital gowns when asked to remove them, as if the staff were just about to play the music and ask them to do the Full Monty for the X-ray department. Many women tense up at the thought that people may be studying their stretch marks or odd stomach flaps and reporting their deeply unsatisfactory findings all over the city.

But when a man is asked to take off his shirt so that someone with a stethoscope can listen to his lungs, that's what they are actually doing, listening to his lungs. They are not measuring him up as an understudy for Schwarzenegger, or checking out his swelling biceps and manly shoulders, and finding him wanting.

"Yes, the medical examination does seem just further indignity"

When a woman removes her clothes to place her breast into the contraption that will deliver a mammogram she is not being auditioned for a *Playboy* centrefold, she is wisely getting herself tested for pre-cancerous cells.

A man who suspects he may have a prostate or hernia problem cannot be examined for either while in his city clothes. A woman can hardly have a smear test while wearing the baggy leggings of her pink track suit.

Yes, the medical examination does seem just one further indignity, inviting humiliation and vulnerability, at the very time when it's least tolerable. None of us would choose to have to show to complete strangers the parts of ourselves that most other human eyes don't reach. But they have seen all those bits of people before. In fact they are seeing such bits all day long.

When we realise that self-consciousness is self-obsessiveness, it's much easier to take off our clothes as quickly as possible and get whatever it is done.

I speak from the point of view of someone not at all satisfied with a body image, but lucky enough to know it's of no interest to anyone on earth except myself. I was helped by a happy childhood where we were all told we looked great and believed it, and by good friends along the way who were never part of any style police.

But I think I was also greatly helped by going to a nudist colony by accident. I was going as a journalist to write about it, and I turned up on the bus with my clothes on, intending to leave them on. But the bus went, and either I took my clothes off or I sat on the side of the road for eight hours until another bus came back to find me. It was in Yugoslavia and it was very hot. I took my clothes off.

I went into the camp and hid behind a bush. Then I crept out a bit and sat sort of covering myself with my handbag on my lap and my arms across my chest, smoking in a frenzy.

And then slowly I noticed people with the most horrific shapes and dangling bits and extraordinary appendages going by, and nobody was paying a blind bit of notice. So I got the courage to slink along the wall towards the restaurant.

I joined the regular campers, and we sat in cafés all day with bits of us falling into the soup, and our bottoms roasting on hot seats. Occasionally we fell into the sea without having to put on or take off swimming costumes. And eventually my eyes stopped looking at the white bits of people and I just got on with the day like everyone else.

It was about the most liberating thing I ever did. I would wish the same sense of freedom to all those I see covering themselves and refusing to come out from behind screens. Who do they think is running some kind of check on them? Why do they think their individual bodies would be of such interest to other people? And that's only in Out-Patients. By the time you get them into a hospital bed there's a whole new set of neuroses.

A lot of these are bedpan-orientated. Again, it's

only natural to be slightly embarrassed that what is usually done in the privacy of a bathroom has to be done in a container in bed and the results removed by someone else.

I made official enquiries about what was the very best thing patients could do about this from a nurse's point of view. The answer was unanimous. They didn't want any theatrics over the bedpan. It was part of their work, people who couldn't move from bed had to have them.

Politeness was always acceptable, and nurses like everyone else always appreciated a word of thanks. But apologies were out of place. It was like trying to deny bodily functions, which was idiotic. As one nurse said very succinctly to me when, like everyone, I apologised for having to use a bedpan, 'Look at it this way, Maeve, if I weren't washing your bottom I'd be washing someone else's'. Which indeed was undeniable.

WHAT'LL YOU HAVE?

I've found six non-alcoholic drinks that taste fine just as long as you don't think they are anything other than what they are. The whole secret is not trying anything that pretends to taste remotely like a real drink.

1) Chilled consommé, served in a glass with freshly ground pepper and a slice of lemon.

2) Alcohol-free lager mixed with orange juice and lemon juice, decorated with slices of orange.
3) Angostura Bitters in a big glass filled up with tonic water and a slice of lime on top.
4) Tomato juice with a little Tabasco, served with a topping of finely chopped red peppers.
5) Strawberries and melon blended together and served in a small glass with fresh mint.
6) Iced coffee in a big glass mug served with a big scoop of ice cream on top.

RELAX ... LET THEM LOOK AFTER YOU

Why must the show go on?

There really is no good reason. If you're ill, recovering from an illness or operation, or just not able to cope for a bit, this is the time to call in the troops.

We must all try to break the habit of a lifetime, thinking we can deal with everything, and instead decide we should allow those who are concerned about us to do something to help. People actually *like* to be told what they can do if they offer to help. They are always offering, begging you to think of something they could do for you at this time. Suppose you were to say to people that there really were a few jobs which would be a huge help? Aren't you truly delighted to do something to help someone else?

In fact, if we're brutally honest, we would all prefer

to do one fairly specific thing to help, rather than to sign on for life as a slave. So a truly thoughtful patient might just think up a list of ten little jobs for the ten people who had offered to help. They would then be overjoyed, and feel important and indispensable. You'd be doing them a favour. You could ask someone to:

Cut the grass.
Do the ironing.
Take out the rubbish bins.
Make you a soup.
Take the hound for a walk.
Vacuum the floor.
Defrost the fridge.
Paint your nails.
Go to the bookies.

And a million other things you can think of while you rest and recover your strength.

9

FIVE THINGS YOU CAN SAY TO ANNOY THE PATIENT IN THE NEXT BED

1) 'Oh, was that your husband? I thought it was your son.'
2) 'Very wise of you not to have too many visitors.'
3) 'Will they be bringing you in a proper dressing gown at all?'
4) 'Would you like this book someone gave me? It's pure rubbish. I can't bear it myself.'
5) 'You were talking in your sleep last night; I hope you don't talk like that when you're at home with your wife!'

HOSPITAL HORROR STORIES

There's some awful, deep-seated thing in people that makes them tell you hospital horror stories when you're not well.

There's a kind of one-to-ten horror scale about these stories:

1) The hospital that was so high-tech no one understood anything.
2) The hospital that was falling down with old age.
3) The woman who was asked her age in front of everyone by a young pup in a white coat.
4) The nurse who behaved like a weasel because her romance was over.

Most people want the nurse to come home with them

5) The man who left his false teeth beside the bed
   and they were tidied away permanently.
6) The radiography department where they lose all
   the X-rays.
7) The time it took an hour for someone hacking
   about to find a vein to draw blood.
8) The hospital where they amputated the wrong leg.
9) The person who went in with one thing and came
   out with something much, much worse.
10) Something that was mis-diagnosed as trivial
    turned out to be fatal.

All of this is total nonsense. And worse, it is inappropriate nonsense. If you were prepared to listen you would hear equally insane horror stories from people about banks, garages, universities, cafés, airports and supermarkets. But you don't feel so vulnerable in these places. You're inclined to believe the gloom merchants when they talk about the horrors connected with illness. Why should you? The hospital has worked fine until now, why should it fall apart the day that you come in?

You will meet fine good people in hospital. Trust me. They're well trained; they don't flap in an emergency; they don't faint when they see blood; they are mainly in this business because they do actually *care* about other people, and there is one sure thing about the nurses . . . they certainly are not in it for the money.

It is, in fact, very reassuring to be among professionals who know what is serious and who realise what definitely is only our own imagination working overtime. They speak soothingly. If you tell them you're frightened and anxious, they won't tell you to pull yourself together and develop a stronger backbone.

Think positive. In hospitals they make you better. That's meant to be – and is – their job.

That nurse is not a weasel. That nurse is probably a sort of angel. The nurse knows how bad it is not to feel well since a nurse's whole working life is spent dealing with exactly such people. Most people fall in love with a nurse or at least want that nurse to come home with them after the hospital stay.

If you go into hospital full of dire forebodings then you'll surely find something that might live up to your gloomy expectations. Instead you should say very firmly on Day One that you have been told no kinder human beings exist on planet Earth than nurses, and no more worthy institutions were invented than hospitals.

Try to believe it, because it's really almost true, and also try to say it in normal, sane, non-babbling tones. You'll wonder afterwards why you listened for two seconds to the horror and doom people.

EIGHT TERRIFIC THINGS TO DO ABOUT GETTING OLD

1) Tie your glasses around your neck and your hearing aid to your ear and your stick to your chair. These are all great gadgets that make life much easier. We should all have had them years ago. The only annoying thing about them is losing them or letting them fall. So don't let that happen – tie them down.

2) Say getting old is challenging – never apologise about it. If you sit clamped in your chair as if you were tied down and padlocked, that's how people will see you. Instead keep reminding them that Paul Newman said, 'Old age ain't for sissies'. It's cool to have Paul in your corner.

3) Demand to be heard on the excellent grounds that you have been around longer than other people and more just might have rubbed off on you from sheer longevity.

4) Tell outrageous, scurrilous and mainly imaginary stories about well-known people long dead and unable to deny it all.

"If you sit clamped in your chair as if you were tied down and padlocked, that's how people will see you"

5) Be eccentric. You're allowed now. Wear the cowboy hat and the feather boa that you've ached to wear for decades but were afraid people would think you looked silly in.

6) Tell everyone you are ten years older than you are. If you say you are seventy-five when you are actually sixty-five people will unaccountably be overcome with admiration. Never for a moment pretend to be younger.

7) Cultivate the friendship of very young people, your grandchildren and your friends' grandchildren. Tell them how idiotic and confused their parents were at their age, and what frighteningly awful haircuts they had.

8) Don't say everything was better in the old days, because it will only make you sound like a boring old fusspot. And really and truly, everything wasn't better, you know.

FIVE WAYS TO RAISE YOUR ANXIETY LEVELS IN HOSPITAL

1) Realise that the running of your home has totally collapsed to the point where your family have put it up for sale, refusing to be comforted; your cats and dogs are yowling to the moon, and the office is in complete chaos.

2) Decide that even worse than this, there is the possibility that everyone and everything is getting on perfectly fine without you.

3) If people don't come to see you, send cards or enquire, accept and believe that they always hated you and this is just the proof you needed.

4) If people do come to visit, accept it's because they heard you are terminally ill, or are guilty at having had an affair with your spouse.

5) If the hospital staff are young, shrewdly deduce that they are therefore raw and inexperienced, and if they are mature, that they are doddering and over the hill.

Your family has refused to be comforted

HIDING BEING LAME

I spent two years of my life hiding the fact I was
lame. Why? Because I foolishly feared that people
might think I was over the hill and not give me work
any more. And because I didn't want endless discus-
sion about it and pity.

So how did I hide it? Mainly by being in places
much earlier than anyone else so that they didn't see
me limp in. If I was meeting people in a café, I
would be well-installed before they arrived, and then
let them leave ahead of me, pretending I had more
work to do, or calls to make before I left, so they
wouldn't see me limping out.

I used to look at each short journey to be made
and work out how many litter bins there were along
the street. They are truly great things to sit on, and
you can always pretend you are studying a map or
reading a paper.

If I were invited to a function in a public place
I'd telephone in advance and ask if I could have a
barstool to sit on. If I were invited to a private house
where people were expected to stand I would ask if
they had a kitchen stool and perch myself on it in a
nice handy area where it was possible to talk to
everyone. I would ask people to my place rather than
go to theirs.

I learned, and then immediately demanded that
all my friends learn, to play bridge, which was nice
and sedentary and no one knew whether you were

lame or not. If ever I was going to stay in a hotel,
I would write and say it didn't matter what kind
of room it was as long as it was near the lift. In a
theatre or a cinema I would ask for an aisle seat near
the back row.

If I hadn't hidden it properly, and on a rare, insen-
sitive occasion anybody asked me why I was limping,

18

I gave some totally unlikely explanation like a skiing accident, a fall from a trapeze, or a sexual experiment with a chandelier that had somehow misfired. It amused nobody but myself really, but no one ever asked again.

One way to hide a little lameness

BE A FRIEND TO YOUR FEET

A quarter of the 206 bones in your body are in your feet.

HOW TO BE HILARIOUS
ABOUT MAKING A WILL

When I was twenty-one my father gave me £100 and
asked me to make a will. Well, I don't think I ever
enjoyed anything as much in my whole life. I sat in
my bedroom sucking a pencil and bequeathing away
all day long.

First I left my mother and father £40 each, which
was an enormous amount of money then, and I
wondered what they would do with it. My mother
might have had a coach tour in Scotland. My father
might have bought some nice bound books. I would
leave my brother and two sisters and Agnes who
lived with us £2 each, which would have bought
them each a very nice treat and totally got them over
the annoyance of losing me from the earth. And I
was going to leave £2 to the cats' home to thank
it for providing us with Smokey, the noble and
admirable half-Persian cat who had stalked through
our youth without giving the slightest sign of
recognising any of us and taught us all whatever
independent streak we have.

But then there was a problem. There would only
be £10 left. I wanted to leave £1 each to my friends
and £1 to an enemy to make her feel remorseful that
she hadn't been much nicer to me. But I had twelve
friends, so there wouldn't be enough. And suppose,
even more worryingly, that I had actually spent some
of my inheritance so that there wouldn't be enough

on the day of reckoning? What would they do then? Interestingly it never crossed my mind that there might be any more than the £100.

I told my father that it was actually a great responsibility having to dispose of £100 justly and honourably and he sighed and told me that indeed it was. I didn't want to take away the enormous legacies that I was giving to my parents. I couldn't bear them to think I had been a cheapskate. And I didn't want to short-change the family or friends either.

So eventually it came to me that if I were to give people percentages, things would work out fine. I wrote my will out in that form.

I knew you had to get it witnessed by two people

who were not going to benefit from it, and they didn't have to know all the secrets you had in it, just to see you signing it was enough. I chose a couple whom I knew only slightly and brought my will along to them. I told them they wouldn't be getting anything themselves in the way of a legacy, but since they worked in the local coffee house and saw that I was often pushed for the price of a cappuccino, I don't think this came as any major disappointment to them.

And so my first will was made. During the next year the enemy left the country, two friends sort of faded away and I had three new ones. I also had a notion of leaving a small sum to the zoo so they would name an owl after me. It was time to make a new will, and I attacked it with gusto.

As I do every year. I have never been afraid of making wills – I love it. A very wise lawyer friend of mine once wrote that the only occasion when making a will might hasten your death is in the pages of an Agatha Christie novel.

Making a will empowers you. You can feel all generous, warm, giving and organised without having to give up a single thing. I have left my gold chain to a Scottish friend who once admired it, and I feel terrifically kind and decent every time I put it on, without ever having to let it out of my grasp.

You should never decide to make a will when you are on the way to the airport, about to take your first bungee jump, or in the middle of a paroxysm of coughing. You should make a will when you feel just fine. You should also tell all your friends to make wills, too. I've shamed a great many people into it by saying in an aggrieved tone that I have left them marvellous things and will be deeply affronted if it turns out that they have left me nothing. Stress that you only want a keepsake, not the deeds of their house. That should reassure them and force them into will-making mood.

When it's all written out in ordinary English you could go to a lawyer who will put in jargon for you. But you can just buy printed forms, and the home made versions are fine, too.

Never start to brood darkly about the words 'Last Will and Testament'. Think, this one is the last one until the next time.

NOTES ABOUT WILLS

Don't say 'If I die'. We all do somtime, as it happens. Say 'When I die' or 'After my death'.

Don't say 'I leave all my money'. That could mean the £10 in your wallet. Instead refer to it as your 'estate'.

Say where things are – 'I leave all the Gene Pitney tapes, which are in a box under the stairs . . .'

Say something schmaltzy and feel-good. I have left a decanter to someone with the sentence: 'In memory of all the happy bottles of wine we shared together'.

Finding your will is not meant to be a game of hide-

and-seek. Leave it in the bank, or your desk, somewhere the beneficiaries won't need radar or sniffer dogs to detect it.

TO PREVENT HYSTERICS

Caraway seeds, finely pounded with a small proportion of ginger and salt, spread upon bread and butter and eaten every day, especially early in the morning and at night before going to bed, is a good remedy against hysterics.

(*The Housewife's Receipt Book*, 1837)

GADGETS FOR THE WISE

A lot of the aids advertised in catalogues for the disabled or indeed the elderly, and available in stores, are extraordinarily useful for those who as yet have no official need for them. It's a wise person who becomes familiar with such items ahead of the posse.

– A safety rail for the shower. You might not need it to hang onto yet, but it's very helpful when you're washing your hair and are blind as a bat.

that's not really what the pick-up stick is meant for – Dear!

- Those bookholder things they have for recipe books also work splendidly for your ordinary reading.
- A piece of strong ribbon or a scarf tied to the car door handle, so that you can pull it shut without straining.
- A one-hand tray that has a kind of basket handle is terrific for going out to the garden or just upstairs.
- Long-handled shoehorns and elastic shoelaces make good sense at any age.
- Velcro fastenings are a hell of a lot easier than buttons in the places that are hard to reach.
- Raised flowerbeds. Have them in the garden *now*, not later. You can always lean on them with a drink in your hand and do a bit of absent-minded gardening.
- A 'goods upwards' box or basket on the bottom step saves on trips upstairs, where it becomes a 'goods downwards' receptacle for things that want to descend.
- A long-handled dustpan is a joyous thing. You'll wonder why they ever made the other kind.
- A pick-up stick is a delightful tool for anything from reaching a hard-to-get book from a high shelf to picking up a piece of newspaper that has blown away.

WHEN CHILDREN ARE SICK

I loved being sick when I was young because I got even more attention than usual. I was allowed to have the big radio in my room, plugged into the wall and standing on a chair. There was a siphon of red lemonade just for me. Nothing was too much trouble and there was huge concern and sympathy.

And of course, I always knew that I would get better eventually, hopefully in time for a party and not in time for the maths exam. For children there is none of that awful 'wondering what it is' business about being ill. They don't go through a mental checklist imagining every headache to be a brain tumour and every wheeze inoperable lung cancer, so in a way they are luckier than the rest of us. All they have to do is put up with the symptoms and wait for them to pass.

But nothing is as stomach churning for parents as looking at a sick child; they are so vulnerable and so different to their normal noisy selves. Had I been a mother myself, I think I never would have survived a child's illness. I'd definitely have needed oxygen just watching whooping cough, and I feel sure I'd have been the one that had to be admitted into Intensive Care if there were an accident of any kind.

Which is why I so admire the way that all the parents I know do cope. They seem to think that the scratches and scrapes and bruises and to my mind near death experiences just go with the territory. Are parents much better and calmer these days? They were certainly more alarmist years ago. Every summer when we went on our seaside holiday there were huge warnings about how dangerous the coast was, and indeed it was true; somebody drowned every summer at that resort. Whenever the cry went up that there was a swimmer in difficulties, every mother and father looked around in blind panic for their own brood, and when they found their children sitting harmlessly making sand-castles a few feet away they often went up and beat the arms and legs off them out of sheer relief. Which seemed very unreasonable, to say the least.

Today's parents seem to me much less flustered. I know a mother who starts to wail whenever her son has a cut knee. She makes such a fuss that eventually he stops crying himself to reassure her that everything is all right.

I know a father who tells his children that a fall from a bicycle or a cut knee is not important in itself but it does involve a lowering of blood sugar. This is pronounced very seriously as in a medical diagnosis, and the solution is proposed that to raise it again all that is required is a square of chocolate. This isn't offered as a distraction or a bribe to stop crying, but as a proven medical remedy. Together they wait to see if it has worked, and soon the hurt child will agree that the blood sugar is back to normal and life can go on.

I was minding an eight-year-old who got up suddenly and unexpectedly from a game of Chinese checkers and went out and vomited. He was perfectly fine. I was the one who was certain he had meningitis or food poisoning and was practising how to tell his parents that he had died in my care. But of course he had been brought up by people who panicked much less than I did.

'Don't worry,' he reassured me. 'It's just that the body doesn't like something so it's sending it back.'

There's a mother who congratulates her children on getting measles or chicken-pox as if they had won some kind of race: 'Aren't you great, you've got it at nine, I was twelve before I got it'. And they feel vaguely triumphant.

For most children, a long-term illness is one that means a week off school. They don't worry about the future the way we would. An accident is just a tree, a gate or a wall that was in the wrong place, not a sign that they are getting feeble and becoming geriatric.

And children just assume that other people who know about such things will cure the problem. We have a lot to learn from them.

THINGS NEVER TO ASK A CHILD

Aren't you a lovely big girl?
Are you a good little boy?
What's your favourite subject at school?
Don't you remember me?
Do you know you have chocolate all round your
    mouth?
Will you give me a kiss goodbye?

Aren't you
a lovely big
girl!

MAKING A FRIEND OF
BLOOD PRESSURE

We should all think very positively about this whole business of having blood pressure taken.

It doesn't hurt.
There are no needles involved.
You don't see any blood.
It's only being done to find out if there is a danger of a heart attack or stroke.
It's just somebody putting a bandage on your arm and squeezing tightly.
It measures the highest pressure (systolic) of the heart's beat and also the lowest pressure (diastolic). Learn those two words just to show off.
They like it to be 130 over 80. That's 130 systolic and 80 diastolic. But that's just perfectionist. It will probably be a bit different.
Don't worry.
The solution is little pills.
You might have to take them all your life. They're no trouble.
Almost half the people you know are taking them.

Of course, if it's too high they'll tell you a few things like:
Stop smoking.
Cut down the alcohol.
Mind your diet.

Take more exercise.
Cut out the salt.

But you *knew* all that, didn't you?

HOW TO BE LESS NERVOUS

When I was young I used to pretend to be brave because I was big, and big people aren't ever allowed to be afraid. Somehow we were meant to be able to cope single-handed at the age of seven with the great hound with slavering jaws that I always thought was around the next corner.

I was afraid to go to England in case I might be eaten by a snake because St Patrick hadn't banished them from there, and I was distinctly worried in case I looked up into a tree, saw a vision and became a saint and quite possibly a martyr, since the two often went together.

I was afraid of the dark and hated going upstairs in case a terrible monster was lurking in the box room. I was afraid to climb a tree in case I fell, I was afraid whenever I saw the doctor in case he might think I needed an injection or vaccination against something. I was terrified that the dentist would get distracted by something else and drill through my head. I watched buses and lorries carefully in case they suddenly left the road and ploughed into me.

Whenever I saw an ambulance or fire engine I thought it was going to our house. I had read somewhere about a European royal family having some disease which meant if they started to bleed they never stopped; I thought I might have it too, so feared it was curtains if I cut myself at all.

I jumped four feet at a loud noise; I thought the sound of leaves in the wind was a burglar; I feared a tidal wave coming in and submerging Dublin. I was always looking at the sky edgily in case a comet was coming towards us, and I thought I saw the Devil on four totally separate occasions.

All in all I was a bag of nerves as a child and yet I grew up into a fairly fearless, reckless kind of adult. But because I remember what it was like to be utterly terrified of almost everything, I am actually most sympathetic to those who think people are drilling into their homes and will come up through the floor any minute, or that they will be beaten to a pulp by the first people they meet if they are mad enough to go abroad.

How did I get the courage of a lion and stop whimpering? Well, first because of something my father once said as we looked at Smokey, the totally deranged cat, creeping around stalking an autumn leaf which was frightening him to death.

My father said it was natural for all animals including humans to have this sense of fear. Otherwise we'd walk into the most desperate situations and wouldn't survive, and that's why our hearts started to race and our breathing began to get fast, and that this was called a state of fight or flight. I found this very cheering, since I had recently been having a bit of a problem with shadows on a bus shelter which I had been fairly sure were escaped gorillas.

I checked it out with my mother. She had been a nurse and was always more graphic about things than other people. She said that when we were frightened every pore in the body opened and let out gallons of sweat. The thinking was that if we were all sweaty then it made us difficult to be grabbed by anything that was pursuing us, if anything was, which it usually wasn't.

She said that this was the reason our hair stood on end too: more difficult to pick up and walk off with something bristling, I suppose. We agreed that it probably wasn't as useful a response nowadays, when humans weren't all covered from head to toe with hair as they used to be. Still the principle was the same, and the old nervous system hadn't quite understood or caught up on how things had changed.

And somehow that helped me a lot. I realised there weren't any gorillas behind the bus shelter. The reason I was so afraid wasn't that I was a coward at all, it was only years of heart-racing and pore-sweating and hair going bolt upright.

So I got cured. It also helped that I realised I couldn't have a good time in life if I was going to be afraid of everything, and I was mad keen to have a good time.

And so the gorillas slunk home, the tidal waves receded, the hostile comets stayed where they were in

Escaped gorillas at the bus shelter

space, and even the aeroplanes seemed safe when you read the statistics. Not everyone is able to have such enlightenment at the age of fourteen, but it could work at any age.

And the facts are all correct. I checked it out recently in a biology book for you. Not as clearly explained as here, of course; a lot of stuff about the autonomic nervous system. But the bottom line is that though it's normal to feel afraid, almost all of the time there are no gorillas or snakes or personal appearances of Lucifer. There is only the poor old over-reacting system that hasn't quite worked it out yet.

THE NERVES OF YOU

Your body has forty-five miles of nerves.

YOU AND YOUR DOCTOR

Remember the doctors are all on your side.
If you want to get better, have nothing to hide.

The doctors have heard every story before –
They will not keel over, and show you the door.

When asked do you drink, then you must not be shy –
Admit that you'd drink any harbour quite dry.

If they ask about cigarettes, don't make a joke.
Don't say a few puffs, if it's fifty you smoke.

Doctors are often obsessed about diet.
If you eat like a glutton, then don't keep it quiet,

But tell the bad news about chocolate and fries –
It's not going to come as a total surprise.

If you think you'll forget the things that they tell,
Try writing them down in a notebook as well.

Doctors can't be clairvoyants, you have to explain
Just where you are feeling the ache or the pain.

Say what tablets you're on, and if you are able,
Bring in the right bottle, its name on the label.

Though their writing is hopeless, they're really quite
   kind –
They're doing their best the solutions to find.

FOR A BRUISED EYE

Take conserve of red roses and rotten apple in equal
quantities, wrap them in a fold of old linen and
apply it to the eye; it will relieve the bruise and
remove the blackness.

(*The Complete Servant*,
Samuel and Sarah Adams, 1825)

HOW TO BE A GOOD FRIEND
TO SOMEONE WHO IS
MENTALLY ILL

If your sister, father, friend or lover doesn't have a
physical illness but a mental one, bunches of grapes,
expensive soaps and heavy helpings of good-natured
common sense might not be at all appropriate.

It goes without saying that as a good friend you
will

…make sure you are available for them and say so.
…help them to find and urge them to stick with professional help.
…never tell them to pull themselves together or to
cheer up.
… stay alert for any signs of possible self-destruction.
…keep cheerful, show no signs of panic and give no
analysis whatsoever.

Mental illness is less terrifying these days, in one respect anyway: at least today it is generally accepted as being just that – an illness which can more and more often be successfully treated.

Those who suffer from the distressing symptoms of a mental disorder don't have to try to hide as they did when sufferers were considered insane because mental illness bore a stigma. Nowadays at least, we have all known so many people who have recovered due to counselling, therapy and medication that such old-fashioned views are no longer current.

Most people I know who have had a mental illness talk about it, and so do their families and friends, which surely must be a healthier way to go on. But even so we don't always get it right for them. And there are things that I have learned from friends who have been through serious depressions, things I would certainly, despite all good intentions, not have known.

It's not a great idea, for example, to keep suggesting things that would cheer you up, automatically thinking they will cheer them up. They might not feel ready or willing to take on a film and supper in a noisy restaurant, but will go out of sheer guilt because you are being so kind. In fact, you could be adding to their misery. Depressed people are not being deliberately obstinate when they refuse to come out; but it would take the pressure off them if they were allowed instead to suggest the activity, and only when they feel up to it.

Sometimes too, meaning well, you can tell a friend

in distress you know exactly how it feels. This is not a real help to someone in a serious or clinical condition. You don't know how it feels. In the end they're only words. If you knew how it felt, you'd be feeling the same way. It's better to ask them to talk to you about what they are feeling, and to stay calm even though what's said might be sad, bleak and alarming. It's more help than what we might mean as words of comfort, but which come across as meaningless platitudes.

Don't tell anyone who is depressed about someone else's depression and how it was conquered. This is at best empty and irrelevant, and at worst it is seen as a betrayal. If you are blabbing and speaking lightly about another person's depression, will you do the same in this case?

It's not always good to cast aside and reject apologies either. Someone who is suffering mental distress might keep saying to friends and relations, 'I'm so sorry for being like this, and leaning on you so much'. Sometimes they just want to apologise, to show that even from the black pit of despair they do know they are being tiresome, repetitive and by your standards, unreasonable.

In this situation, a lot of people have found that it's better to simply accept the apologies. You might just say you know they're sorry and know they're not in any way at fault. At least that way you are acknowledging the fact that despite their own pain they realise they are causing you anxiety or upset or difficulties of one kind or another. This is better than dismissing any expression of regret or insisting their behaviour is absolutely normal or no trouble at all, which they know is not the case.

Humour is not always out of place in such conversations. Not stand-up comedy or set pieces, but people who suffer from depression have told me they love bleak and even black jokes. This obviously won't be right for everyone, but for a few, it's a relief.

AN ELEGANT MEDICINE CUPBOARD

For some reason people always peep into your medicine cupboard. Fool them totally. Have lovely fresh-looking things in it with no sign of suppositories, false teeth fixative, violent laxatives or unmerciful cures for diarrhoea. Instead have:

- harmless-looking vitamins.
- hangover cures to show what a racy life you lead.
- some essential oils for aromatherapy.
- a small whip that will have them speculating about you for years.

Put the things you really need in a different box entirely. Cover it with a nice towel and leave it as a little stand for the lavatory brush. Nobody will dream of investigating it.

ELASTIC STOCKINGS

These are terrible things which apparently are hugely beneficial. Nobody ever tells you about them in advance so I thought I would warn you.

They are to stop clots which might form if your legs were to be allowed to roam free, and somehow they are meant to hold you together after operations, or ease your varicose veins, which is all very admirable and much to be desired. They don't hurt at all when they're on. In fact, they actually feel very comfortable when they're in place.

That's all the good news.

The bad news is that it's like having a skin graft putting them on and taking them off. You see someone approaching, holding this unyielding white cloth container which looks as if it wouldn't fit over your thumb let alone over your whole leg, and you grit your teeth.

But first the stocking that is already on has to come off. You'd be afraid to look in case most of your flesh had gone with it, but amazingly your poor leg looks intact. Sad and white, but still all there.

You remember the times when you didn't have this ritual every day and you wonder why you didn't feel ludicrously carefree and happy from dawn to dusk.

It's no use suggesting, as I did, that maybe you don't need to wash your legs all that much, and that possibly you could keep the elastic stockings on for a week or so. They don't like that as a notion.

"How to pull on and take off Elastic stockings"

It sounds filthy and disgusting. No use offering the theory that your poor old legs couldn't really get very dirty just lying in bed going nowhere. They hate that as a theory. Legs just have to be washed every day, that's it. And they can't be washed through stockings, so you have to have the things removed and replaced daily.

I used to hate this more than anything else in hospital, more than giving blood, getting blood, going through that scanning machine, which was very expensive apparently, and where I always thought I would get stuck because I was too chubby and they would have to sacrifice me or the machine.

43

But bad and all as it was having the elastic stockings put on and taken off by kind, trained hospital staff, it was totally horrific trying to do it at home.

In theory – in someone's mad theory – you are meant to be able to do it yourself. It's all a matter of getting the heel in the right place and then pulling the stocking up with a pick-up stick.

That doesn't work. The heel is never in the right place and the pick-up stick keeps losing the stocking or tearing it. You really need the services of a good kind spouse, partner, relative, friend, or passer-by. Someone firm enough to refuse to let you grow fungus on your legs by allowing you some days' respite between the changes. Someone technical enough to work out the amazing geometry of getting the heel on first. Someone kind enough to put up with all the ungrateful yelps and groans. Someone far-sighted and optimistic enough to realise that this is unlikely to be forever, who realises that one blissful day the authorities will allow you to let your legs run free again.

TEN GIFTS MOST PATIENTS WOULD LOVE

1) A dozen stamped postcards to write short thank-you letters or accounts of their ailments to the outside world.
2) A laptop tray, a thing with a flat top and a bean bag bottom, which doesn't slide off the bed.

Something to make him feel more desirable

3) An artificial silk flower that won't eat the oxygen, need any water, annoy the nurses, or die and upset everyone.
4) A bar of ludicrously expensive designer soap that no one would ever buy in real life.

5) The loan of a Walkman or tape recorder and three talking books.
6) A bottle of really good salad dressing or vinaigrette. Hospital food can be very bland; this cheers up almost everything but the semolina.
7) Gossipy and silly magazines. Energetic sporting, mountaineering and boxing publications can make the weak feel weaker still.
8) For women: a pinkish scarf to drape around the shoulders is inclined to make the greyest face look a bit more lively.
9) For men: a small bottle of expensive cologne to slap around his chops and make him feel more desirable.
10) Some vague proof, in the form of a card with many signatures on it, that friends, family, neighbours or colleagues have not forgotten the patient.

REMEDIES AGAINST FLEAS

Fumigation with brimstone or the fresh leaves of pennyroyal sewed in a bag and laid on the bed will have the desired effect.

(*The School of Arts, or Fountain of Knowledge*, Mrs de Salis, 1890)

HEAD TO TOE EXAMINATION: A FEW MORE THINGS TO WORRY ABOUT

You have far too much hair and look like a monkey

You have too little hair and will shortly go totally bald

Your eyes are too wide open, making you look mad and staring

You have drooping eyelids and look like a criminal and a vulture

Your tongue is white and unhealthy looking

Your tongue is red and dangerous looking

Your bosom is too small and flat and dull

Your bosom is too big and floppy and disappointing

Your skin is oily and greasy and full of harmful impurities

Your skin is dry and flaky and about to fall off in chunks

Your private parts are small, pathetic and insignificant

Your private parts are huge, obviously deformed and revolting

Your knees are weak and give way all the time

Your knees are stiff and unyielding

Your feet are hard and scaly and disgusting

Your feet are soft and mushy and disgusting

SENIOR DECISIONS

Years ago I had this great notion, which was that together with all our friends we should go into an old people's home long before we were really old, but while we were young enough to enjoy it. It seemed the perfect solution to everything.

We would all sell our houses and take a wing together. We would hire a part-time waiter to bring us gins and tonics on a tray with a folded white table napkin over his arm. We would be looked after, we would have company, we could move from room to room playing bad bridge. We could take over a lounge for ourselves and have parties. We wouldn't have to worry about our friends coming to see us because they would all be there.

If we had children and grandchildren, nephews and nieces, they would be delighted not to have to worry about us as we got feebler. They could have all our furniture and our treasures now rather than later. They would visit us because we would all be such fun, growing older without a care in the world.

We wouldn't be tormented with fear of losing our keys, or burglars or conmen or burst pipes or setting the house on fire or getting malnourished, because the home would look after all that side of things.

We would have no sense of being beached, no lingering resentment that we should possibly be living with relations, because after all we chose this ourselves.

It seemed such a flawless idea that we were almost ready to go in straight away. Even though we were decades below the age that one might expect people to consider such a step, we started sussing out places of residential care.

Somebody said that if this was such a great idea why had nobody thought of it before?

And then they all got restless. There had to be a snag in it somewhere.

I was just forty at the time and very keen to go in that year. I couldn't see where the problems were suddenly coming from, so to rid everyone of anxieties I decided to test out the theory by writing an article about the whole idea in the *Irish Times*.

It met with the kind of mild patronising approval which annoyed me intensely. It was as if I were being patted on the head for a silly, off-the-wall, humorous look at the future, while I thought I had sorted out a whole area of angst, potential loneliness and confusion for an entire generation.

We were the people who would provide the smooth transition from the extended family concept, where everyone took in their grandparents automatically, to a world where housing, the economy and society meant that adults made their own arrangements for old age. But nobody was taking me seriously.

And then the two most boring people in the whole country wrote to the newspaper and said they would like to join us in all this, and where would they pay their deposit.

Now, I am very sure that people may well cross roads to avoid talking to me, but these are people who would empty a stadium if they were seen to approach. They could bore at Olympic competitions, bore not just for the nation but for the planet.

In vain did I tell my friends that we didn't have to have them with us. We could tell them politely that the subscription had now closed, that they would have to start their own. This was the whole essence of the idea, I begged them to believe. The idea was that groups of like-minded people should form an ageing commune of their own with people of shared interests.

But the very mention of the two awful and frightening people had destroyed the fragile edifice. My friends kept thinking of how awful it would be if you thought you might meet them at breakfast every single day of your life, or hear them booming around the place with their entirely unacceptable views.

We all decided reluctantly that we would live in our own places until the time came, with no plans, and take whatever happened. So it was over, the dream that might have changed society.

But perhaps some day someone else might reinstate it. A word of warning, however. Just do it quietly. Don't write anything about it in a newspaper.

CHEERING THINGS ABOUT
CHEST PAINS

I once went to a women journalists' conference in Central America where so much went wrong and the stress was so high that if there had been an Intensive Care Unit within miles I think all 600 participants would have been in it.

The hotel booking system was so bad we slept three to a room, and one of my room-mates woke in the night with terrible chest pains. One of the waitresses was a third-year medical student, and since she was all we had, she stood there in her nightie while frightened women in all languages tried to interpret for each other by candle-light, since the generator had gone again.

I hope by now she is an acclaimed heart specialist in her own land, that young girl who reassured everyone in sight. She stood there in the candle-light telling us that it need not be what we all feared.

'You see, the chest she ees a beeg complex structure. The chest, she has many major organs. As well as the heart, the pain could be in these. She has the ribs, and they could be cracked like firewood. The chest, she has the muscles, and these could be strained by too much sex or climbing around the ruins. The chest is also the area where unwisely chosen food could cause the indigestion.'

A little colour was coming back to the face of our room-mate. The banquet – when we'd eventually

"The chest, she ees a beeg, complex structure"

found it – had offered a rather leathery sausage.
Please may this be what it was.

But the waitress was not finished. 'The chest, she
ees so interesting she could hold the pleurisy, the
bronchitis . . .' She beamed at all the things the chest
could hold which might not be a fatal heart attack.

And now, decades later, women from forty coun-
tries have remembered her calm round face, her lack
of fear, her insistence that we didn't all choose the
worst-case scenario. Not only was she right then but

I imagine she has been right for all of us who had a chest pain sometime and were able to call up her wonderful, calming words:

'The chest, she ees a beeg complex structure ... '

HIGH WIND

A sneeze can travel as fast as 100 miles per hour.

CHAIN LETTER FOR WEARY WOMEN

Dear Friend

This letter was started by a woman like yourself in hopes of bringing relief to other tired and discontented women. Unlike most chain letters this one does not cost you anything.

You bundle up your husband, partner or boyfriend and send him to the woman whose name appears at the top of this list. Then add your own name to the bottom of the list and send a copy of this letter to five of your friends who are equally tired and discontented.

When you come to the top of the list you will receive 3,125 men and some of them are bound to be better than the one you gave up.

DO NOT BREAK THIS CHAIN. One woman did and she received her own man back.

WHY I TOOK UP DRINK:
A PERSONAL HORROR STORY

As in everything else, I was a late starter. For one thing, I didn't like the taste. We always had whiskey on a piece of cotton wool to cure a toothache, and it had bad associations. For another, everyone I met who did drink alcohol seemed to be racked with guilt, penniless and feeling very sick indeed. They didn't go on with all this 'never again' thing about cream buns or chocolate or even ten Woodbine. But fellows after too many pints and girls after too many sherries seemed to be in the last stages of remorse. Drink didn't seem to have all that much to recommend it.

Then one day, when I was about twenty-two, I went to a wedding. The bride and groom were an extremely handsome couple. They could have been sent over by Central Casting so much did they look the part.

And as we all followed them glumly out of the church I caught sight of my reflection in a glass door.

Now I hadn't any great illusions about the way I looked. I was wearing a suit belonging to my mother which hadn't looked great on her either, and it had been bundled up in the bicycle shed of the school where I taught.

Why was this, you ask? So I could change into it after I had complained of not feeling well so I could get off my Saturday morning teaching to go to the wedding. I'd also gone to the wedding on the bus without the benefit of a mirror to indicate the unusual shape and angle of a very old hat.

'I look desperate,' I said to a woman beside me.

'I know you do,' she said reassuringly. 'So do I. I can't wait to get into the drink to make me forget it.'

'Will drink make me forget what I look like?' I asked innocently, and began life as a drinker.

I loved drink. Loved it. And I may be wrong but I don't think it turned me into a Jekyll and Hyde. I was just rather louder and even more insanely talkative and cheerful than the norm. I forgot things, of course, and had hangovers and stayed on much too late in places. But what the hell.

And amazingly my liver held out and I didn't lose my job or house or my friends over it. But one day when I couldn't walk or stand or lie down, and most important of all couldn't sleep with arthritis, it was put to me rather plainly that if I were even to think about a new hip then a great deal of weight would have to be lost. And drink, however jolly, and to my mind it is very jolly, is a great enemy of weight loss. It looked, sadly, as if we were into extremes again.

HOW I GAVE UP DRINK: AN INSPIRING STORY

I had a great plan. I would drink one day a month. Every single month there would be an Evening with

Wine. I would plan this carefully for about thirty days.

And I did. The actual outings themselves were fairly spectacular because they were so eagerly anticipated.

In January I went to an Italian restaurant on my wedding anniversary and after two glasses of wine became helpless and incapable with drink and tears. I sobbed to the whole clientele, and eventually to the kitchen staff who came out to know what was happening, how very, very happy I was. I apparently listed all the shortcomings of the people I hadn't married. It took three days to get over that.

In February I had one glass of a very full-bodied red wine in South Africa and more or less passed out until I was assisted to the taxi.

In March I unwisely drank some champagne on a flight to Chicago and fought bitterly with the air stewardess who was going to marry a man she didn't love. I was so depressed by her attitude to things, I brooded too much about it and fell out of bed, breaking my nose and my toe.

In April I was so ashamed of what had happened in March I had no evening at all with wine.

In May it was my birthday so I had an Evening with Wine surrounded by cushions and rugs in case I fell again.

And then in June I had lost the weight and I got the new hip.

Now I know all this sounds very extreme and possibly not at all helpful to normal people. But there just might be a few extreme folk looking at this book who will be helped, which is why I decided to share my inspiring if somewhat overly-dramatic tale.

I have an Evening with Wine once a week now, which isn't nearly as nice as an Evening with Wine every night. But it's four times better than once a month.

"I loved drink. Loved it"

TEN WONDERFUL THINGS ABOUT GIVING UP DRINK

1) You feel heroic.
2) Your liver turns nice and pink again.
3) You won't have to explain. Only the worst kind of bore begs you to 'have just one' these days. Mostly, people actually don't notice if you're drinking or not. Trust me on this, it surprised me too.
4) You don't have hang-overs.
5) You save money.
6) You remember what happened.
7) You get more work done.
8) You won't find it nearly as bad as you think. Anticipating a dry evening is much worse than actual-ly having one, and no wine is easier than a little wine. Trust me on this too.

9) You don't get that that sudden urge to eat every-thing that's on the table.

10) You have a load of great help out there if this advice isn't quite enough for you.

UTTERANCES FROM A HOSPITAL BED THAT WILL ENSURE YOU GET NO MORE VISITS

'I thought you were never going to get here.'

'Oh, it's you again, is it?'

'Well, how do you think I am, stuck in here?'

'Not more fruit, I'll turn into an orange at this rate.'

'I hope you're keeping the place properly at home.'

'I've read that, you can take it home with you.'

'They say I'm getting better, but what do they know?'

'It's easy for you, you can walk away on your own two good legs.'

'You'll never guess what my last visitor brought me . . .'

'You can go now if you want to.'

'You mean you're going already?'

WHERE THINGS ARE

I used to think the kidneys were somewhere in the knickers area. But they're not. They are up behind your bra strap, if you are the sex and shape that wears a bra. If not you still know where I mean.

Get a map of arteries. They look like an amazing underground rail system. We might clog them and fur them a bit less if we knew what they look like.

Be courageous and look at a picture of the large

X.RAY

intestine and the small one. Why should we come over all silly and squeamish about how bits of us look if we expect medical people to take them in their stride?

Examine a picture of a skeleton and see whether the knee bone is actually connected to the thigh bone, etc. or if it's only a song.

If a real medical text on all this is too much for you, get a child's book on the body. The basics are there but presented much more cheerfully.

And why not take a mirror and look into your own orifices? You look into totally unimportant things like other people's windows, open handbags, shopping trolleys in a supermarket. You won't tremble so much about an ear, nose, throat or indeed any other aperture, if you have examined it in good health.

THE DEMON SMOKES:
ONE ADDICT'S STORY

If there was an easy way to give up smoking, I feel pretty sure we would have heard of it by now. In the meantime, there is some research to show that reading other people's stories of renunciation actually paves the way. Here's mine.

I got the whole way through school and college without smoking. And this was despite growing up in a home where most around me were wheezing and inhaling and gasping and either complaining about the cost of cigarettes if they were old enough to buy them or unravelling butts in ashtrays if they weren't.

My friends all smoked and they never once congratulated me on my strength. They just said Maeve was useless because she never had five zipped away in the back of a bag like other nicer people did. I had nothing to offer in a crisis and no way of being calmed down myself by others if the crisis was in my court.

And then one fateful day a particularly horrible acquaintance inhaled through her slim body right down to her tiny feet and told me I was very brave not to smoke.

Brave?

Yes, apparently. Because if I had been smoking, I wouldn't have been eating a warm almond bun covered with butter.

I looked around the group. They were frighteningly elegant. They even made smoke rings, some of them. None of them had fingers covered in butter, none of their eyes were looking at the last almond bun on the plate.

We had all been to a film where Humphrey Bogart and Lauren or Ingrid or some other non-almond-bun-eating person had looked just terrific.

A grown-up sensible woman of twenty-two, earning my own living, not a pre-teen racked with insecurity, I can still hear myself saying to the horrible acquaintance that I'd give it a try.

That was in 1962. For the next sixteen years

"none of them had fingers covered in butter"

nobody saw me much, because I was behind a thick wall of smoke. I suppose I didn't eat as many almond buns as I had, but it didn't really matter since I was hardly visible.

I discovered interesting things, like you could ask a total stranger for a cigarette, which you didn't normally do for a chocolate biscuit, and you couldn't really sleep well if there wasn't a packet beside you.

I wasn't very elegant. I never learned to make smoke rings. There was a lot of ash on my chest, little burns in my tights and I was forever making loud, unpleasant throat-clearing sounds. I fell into habits I had once found disgusting in others, such as crushing butts out in the empty grapefruit rinds on breakfast plates. But what the hell. I was a smoker, and all that sort of thing goes with the territory.

And then, in 1978, there was a bad flu in England. As I lay in bed with a pain in my chest, red-eyed and very self-pitying, I heard a newsreader on the radio say, in tones that managed to be both doom-laden and urgent at the same time, that all over the country, the flu had turned to pneumonia in heavy smokers. Panic-stricken, I leaped from the bed and went to the surgery.

The waiting room was so full that patients were standing in lines around the wall, all of us spluttering and clutching our chests. When my turn came the doctor looked up wearily. It had been a long morning.

He tried to put some sympathy into his greeting

to what may have been the ninetieth person who had sneezed on top of him in the last two hours.

'Flu?' he suggested.

'Pneumonia,' I corrected. 'It's pneumonia, I heard it on the radio.'

Doctors often get patients who have heard messages from the radio or outer space. They are time-consuming people. He looked at me sadly.

'Oh dear,' he said.

I was desperate at this stage. 'Doctor,' I implored, 'I would be the last person to think of mentioning the British Medical Council, but are you or are you not going to listen to my chest?'

In the background, the 150 or so meek and obedient people who would have readily accepted they had flu barked like poor sick seals in the waiting room. To humour me, and mainly to get rid of me, he took out his stethoscope and plonked it in the area of my lungs.

'Breathe in,' he said through clenched teeth.

I did and the pain was desperate.

'What do you hear?' I croaked.

'I hear that you are fat, you are forty and you smoke five packs of cigarettes a day,' he said as he wrote a prescription for antibiotics to deal with post-flu infections.

He was three years on the wrong side of my age, of course, which was fairly offensive. But he was right otherwise.

'You mean the pain has to do with smoking?' I asked in disbelief.

'Oh yes, indeed,' he said and rang the bell for the next patient.

And just because it was all so obvious to him, and because he didn't even try to make me give them up, some kind of scales fell from my poor red eyes and to this day I have never smoked another cigarette.

AIR CONDITIONING

Your nose is busy cleaning, warming and humidifying more than 500 cubic feet of air each day.

AGEING HIPPY

If you have to have a new hip, believe me *nobody* will ever tell you about it as straight as I will.

No technical jargon. No ludicrous, perfectionist advice about keeping fit. Just the facts, explained both simply and graphically.

Hips rot away. I don't know exactly why . . . sometimes it's congenital, sometimes as a result of an injury . . . but anyway, when the ball-and-socket joint that sort of sticks your leg to the trunk of your body starts to decay you feel terrible.

Now don't let anyone get away with the words 'a touch of arthritis'. It's much, much worse. It's as if somebody accidentally left a carving knife in your groin and nobody took it out. And yet somehow, to those who don't know how bad it is, it's seen as some vague rheumaticky sort of ache, originating somewhere mainly in the mind.

It gets worse. You can't walk, you can't stand, you can't sleep. You are old before your time, and you can't go out into the streets and cry aloud how really badly you feel or they will think you are mad as well as rheumaticky.

So you go to a doctor who sends you to get X-rays, and if they show that your hip is in bits, be pleased rather than upset. That means they can do something about it.

Then you see an orthopaedic surgeon, who, if you are lucky, will agree to give you a new hip. This is the moment where you really and truly need my advice. It's in three simple words. Go for it.

This is an operation with a huge success rate. You will wake up and the pain has not only gone . . . it stays gone.

Let me tell you my story.

I was the fattest patient the surgeon had ever met, and he said that even though he could see my poor hip was in smithereens, honestly, I was so fat that if he did my hip I would die on the operating table. If I lost the weight, he said he would think again.

I lost the weight. It was really only possible because I had the carrot of a pain-free life dangling in front of me. I then heard the words that I was to come in for the operation.

I was so excited at first I told everyone. And I was delighted, but of course in the long reaches of the night I wondered was I mad. Fortunately, there

wasn't too much time to brood before I was in there,
lying rigid with terror in a hospital bed in my purple
nightie.

They sort of go over you the night before an
operation to make sure you are a reasonable risk.
Everyone is very cheery and matter-of-fact and you
sign things about knowing what's involved, and naming
your next of kin, and then they say good night.

During the night I got this sudden insight. The insight was that I was mad to be having a new hip, I was fine as I was. So I couldn't sleep, walk, stand, work, think, enjoy anything, but basically I was fine. I must have over-exaggerated my symptoms.

I must go home now, I thought, and crawled out of bed, and found my two walking sticks and my coat.

I had got as far as the door when the nurse came in and guided me firmly back to bed. Lots of people do this, according to the nurse. It's called a night hallucination. I lay there glumly until the trolley came.

They don't give you a tranquilliser as I had thought, so you go down quite awake. The operating theatre looked like something from a television series.

I am a person who thinks that something should be said on every occasion. 'I think I'll leave it all to you,' I said to the surgeon, and they all seemed deeply relieved.

It was an epidural injection, the kind that people often have in labour. I was very afraid I would be awake for it all, and know what they were doing, and try to stop them. But no, completely the reverse. I must have had some kind of nice relaxing drug somewhere along the line, because not only did I feel nothing but also I didn't know where I was.

I thought I was in a hotel, entertaining this group of people around my couch. I talked non-stop for whatever number of hours it took. I said I was so sorry that I had chosen a place with such heavy building going on, all that drilling and hammering, but then, on the other hand, you had to be grateful there was so much building industry going on these days. I had absolutely no idea that the drilling and hammering was all on my own leg.

Then, after a day in Intensive Care, where apparently I wanted to know the full words of 'They Can't Take that Away from Me' and sang tunelessly the bits I remembered, they tell me I was brought back to my own bed and I realised the pain was gone.

So you say it can't be so easy? It is. Why would I lie to you?

In my own case, I had horrible, weak, rotten bones, so it took me a bit longer to get out of bed than the rest of my ward. But I was never competitive.

And there were some amazing things that followed:

... like not being allowed to sleep on your side. There was a horrible contraption in the bed to stop you doing that.
... like the fact that you didn't seem to own your new hip; it was always referred to as the surgeon's new hip.
... like you had to slide his hip to the side of the bed before standing up, or lay his hip carefully on a strange triangular cushion for chairs, or position his hip over a high seat on the lavatory.
... like the really revolting elastic stockings.

... like not being allowed to sit up in bed on your own by moving your bum; instead you had to drag yourself up by this extraordinary gadget that hung over the bed and was meant to develop your arm muscles, I suppose. For those who used it, I suppose it did.

I just snuggled down and read more and more books. Then I was cured and went home.

I am no role model for anyone. I did not do all the horrific exercise they demanded. I just hate the thought of my lungs filling up with all that air and oxygen and everything if it means I have to walk vigorously every day.

But for more than two years I have had no pain whatsoever. I can manage stairs and airports and corridors and I have sleep-filled nights. To me this is reward enough to make me advise anyone else to have the operation.

I know that when my next hip needs replacing I will go in there like a lamb. I will always celebrate the leap of faith in those who knew that arthritis was not just malingering. It was debilitating, destructive and not at all part of a so-called natural ageing process. Their foresight and skills in this area will be forever celebrated.

SOME AMAZINGLY FATTENING THINGS TO EAT

Fried bread
Roast goose with a lot of skin
Tiramisu
Peanut butter sandwich with banana and jam
Sausage roll
Digestive biscuits almost hidden by pâté
Any dessert called 'Special Chocolate Plate'

WHEN IT IS REALLY SERIOUS

I had a friend who was told out of a clear blue sky
that he had only three more months to live. Since he
was someone who had a fair chance of about twenty
or even thirty more years, the shock for him and his
many friends was overwhelming.

But he was the one who handled it extremely well,
it was the friends who floundered. Some were literally
unable to face it at all. They feared going to see him
lest they break down and make things worse, if that
were possible.

Some came with false hopes and cures. There was
much confident talk of the power of crystals, the
hands of a healer, the lichen that grew on some rock
in the desert. Some came with stories of magnificent
surgeons in this city or in that medical centre.

Some sent holding letters, full of vague generalities

about not losing hope and promising a visit they never intended to make. Some – and these, he found, were the saddest – sent him little Get Well cards with pictures of bunny rabbits weeping into a handkerchief and saying 'So sorry to hear that you're sick'.

The other kind of card he got fairly regularly was a jolly vulgar one, with sexual innuendo or bedpan humour and cheerful bluff messages inside saying something like 'Come on now, mate, we are counting on you to beat this'.

And as he lived out his three months calmly he did not rail against those with the inability to say goodbye. He said that until it happened to him he would have done more or less the same, apart from the bunnies crying into the handkerchiefs.

He said that he wasn't at all living twenty-four hours a day in fear and terror of what will, in any event, happen to us all sometime, but in his particular case would happen within a given and short period of time. Having some notice gave you a chance to take stock, he said, and forced you to do those things you had been intending to do for years.

He went to see the Grand Canyon, and stood and watched three magical sunsets there without self-pity because even without his diagnosis, he said, he would probably not have gone back again anyway. He tidied up all his affairs, wrote to public figures whom he had admired. He gave his books and pictures away to people who might like them.

He was low sometimes, but never frightened, and

74

he claimed that he didn't waste one of his eighty-four days on useless regrets. He said the very best thing people could do for him was to visit him at home and give the one obligatory acknowledgement of regret that he was about to die so soon. He said you needed that much, otherwise the conversation was entirely artificial and everyone was in some kind of denial. After that you left it.

He loved people to talk about the world that he had lived in, the people they knew, the social beliefs they had shared or argued over, the successes, the failures, the near disasters, the funny things that had happened along the way, the amount of the twentieth century they had seen together, with all the changes for good and not for good.

He liked the glamorous fifty-something woman who claimed she had always fancied him, safe enough to say now that it was too late, and the tough, pushy businessman who invented a mythical reason to be in the area and came along to learn a three card trick. He told my friend he needed to know how to do 'Find the Lady' before the secret was gone forever.

As for the people who really couldn't visit because of the distance . . . well, it would be great if they could telephone or write a letter, a proper letter, rather than hiding behind a greeting card, he said. Nothing emotional or weepy, but something that might make sense of a life lived and now ending. He said there were some amongst his friends who could do this, but not enough. And he liked to hear that there would be a tree planted here and a rose bush there for him.

He missed the many people that he knew had liked him greatly and were crying for him, and for whom he was already dead because he was no longer in their lives as someone full of hope and future. Unless you are a king in a fairytale, you can't summon people to your deathbed, but he wished they had come.

His story isn't everyone's story, but it just might be many people's. And at least it might make us think twice before automatically reaching for the excuse or worse, a card that purports to say it all and only says we ourselves have no real words of friendship left to offer.

IN AN IDEAL WORLD ...

In an ideal world every patient would be a twinkling, smiling, grateful person propped up with pillows, overcome with gratitude that we have come to visit.

The perfect patient's face will crack open into a huge smile of delight as if no other person on earth could possibly be as welcome as we are. There will be nice fresh fruit on offer, a few chocolate truffles, maybe even books or magazines to lend us because they have already been read and it would be a kindness, really, to clear space in the bedside locker.

Ideally the patient will have no complaints about anything, the prognosis is good, the doctors are inspired, the nurses are angels and the hospital food is fine.

We'd all go hospital visiting if only we could be sure the patients were going to be like that. But there are days when we approach a bed and know that its going to be far from ideal.

I was in a hospital ward and heard a woman greet her daughter who had come in by a horrific journey involving one train and two buses. The mother's first words were that she need not bother to come in again wearing that short skirt and looking like a tart.

I saw a man welcome his white-faced, anxious wife during visiting time by saying that she had yet again brought the wrong sporting paper and was there a chance that one day she might get something right.

I once went to see a fairly feisty, elderly woman who decided that she would prefer to go to sleep than talk to me. Sleep, she explained was one of the few pleasures she had left to her and that she felt a wave of it coming over her at that moment, she was sure I would understand.

I have seen a three-year-old boy coming in to a maternity ward clutching flowers for his mother and what does he find but that she's cradling and cooing over a small screaming, red-faced baby, with no similar hugs for himself. And on top of all this he is meant to be pleased that this horrible thing has joined the family.

And in this perfect world every patient would look out of bed and see a regular stream of delightful, concerned visitors coming to see them carrying exactly the right gift. These ideal visitors would want to know the most detailed minutiae of every happening since they last visited. They would be fascinated by any change in medication, temperature charts, blood pressure levels. They would beg for details of what the consultant said, what the house-man identified and whether the nurse taking blood had found a good sturdy vein. They would remember the names of every single member of staff that had been mentioned. They would bring warm personal greetings from almost everyone in the outer world and give the impression that society as we know it had almost broken down because of the patient's temporary absence in hospital.

But of course that's not going to happen for the poor patient either. It's a far from perfect world.

I must explain that I am an avid reader of self help books. I have shelves of them at home. I truly think that almost everything can be learned from a manual. But if you have hundreds of manuals, as I do, about topics such as how to flatten your stomach, have perfect skin, thrive on stress, play demon bridge or cook with yeast, then you will realise that if you get one single piece of useful information from any manual then you are doing well.

Wendy Shea and I, hopeless but caring and cheerful patients and well meaning hospital visitors in turn, wish just that there may have been *something* in these pages that made you believe that things weren't quite as bad as you thought they would be. Just this one small insight is all we want for you. Then it will have been worth while writing and illustrating this bossy little book.